BRITISH
CLOCKS AND
CLOCKMAKERS

KENNETH ULLYETT

WITH
8 PLATES IN COLOUR
AND
24 ILLUSTRATIONS IN
BLACK & WHITE

LIST OF ILLUSTRATIONS

PLATES IN COLOUR

THIRTY-HOUR STRIKING AND ALARUM BRASS LANTERN CLOCK
Jeffrey Bayley. Signed and dated 1653

THIRTY-HOUR STRIKING HANGING CLOCK IN INLAID
MARQUETERIE CASE
Christopher Gould, c. 1690

EARLY LONG-CASE CLOCKS
Thirty-hour, ten-inch dial clock. Walnut veneer and inlaid boxwood stringing
Thomas Tompion, c. 1675
Second-and-a-quarter clock in inlaid marqueterie case. Thomas Harris, c. 1690
Thirty-hour, portico-top clock in walnut case. Henry Crump, c. 1670

EARLY LONG-CASE CLOCKS
Thirty-hour striking clock with single hand and engraved dial plate. Ebony veneer on oak
case. Early Daniel Quare, c. 1671
Ten-inch dial, striking and alarum clock in marqueterie case. Joseph Windmills, c. 1685
Long-case clock with skeleton silvered hour-ring cut away to show gilt dial. Walnut-veneered
case. John Ebsworth, c. 1690

LONG-CASE CLOCKS OF THE EIGHTEENTH CENTURY
Twelve-inch arch dial clock. Mahogany case. John Ross of Tain, c. 1780
Early arch dial clock. Burr walnut case. Joseph Windmills, c. 1710
Twelve-inch dial month clock with semi-sonniary striking. Daniel Quare, c. 1720

ALARUM AND STRIKING MANTEL CLOCK IN EBONY-VENEERED CASE
Henry Jones, c. 1685

CHIMING MANTEL CLOCK WITH MOON-WORK, IN RED AND GOLD
LACQUER CASE
Thomas Turner, c. 1760

ENGLISH WATCHES
Gold watch with outer case of carnelian. Made by Strigner for James II, c. 1687
Enamelled and jewelled gold watch. David Bouquet, fl. 1628–1665
Gold repeating watch in open-work case. Thomas Tompion and Edward Banger, 1701

BLACK AND WHITE ILLUSTRATIONS

	PAGE		PAGE
Rye Church Clock, 1515 Dial and Quarter-Boys *Photograph by courtesy of the Society of Antiquaries of London*	7	Tavern Clock in Trunk Case, c. 1760 *By courtesy of the Director of the Victoria & Albert Museum*	29
Interior Dial of Wells Cathedral Clock Showing Jousting Knights *Photograph by courtesy of B. C. Phillips, Esq.*	11	Hood of Lacquered Long-Case Clock James Markwick, c. 1720 *By courtesy of the Director of the Victoria & Albert Museum*	30
Nicolaus Kratzer, Astronomer to Henry VIII Oil-painting by Hans Holbein, 1528 Louvre, Paris	13	Hanging Clock Mahogany case with applied carved and gilt decoration, c. 1760 *By courtesy of the Director of the Victoria & Albert Museum*	35
Watch in Case and Cover of Smoke Crystal with Dial of Enamelled Gold Michael Nouwen of London, 1609 *By courtesy of the Trustees of the British Museum*	14	Dead-Beat Escapement Model of the escapement invented by George Graham, c. 1715 *By courtesy of the Director of the Science Museum*	37
Striking Clock in Engraved Silver-Gilt Case Bartholomew Newsam, c. 1590 *By courtesy of the Trustees of the British Museum*	15	Christopher Gould's Signature Engraved on the hanging clock, illustrated in the colour plate facing page 9	38
Jeffrey Bayley's Signature Engraved on the brass lantern clock illustrated in the colour plate facing page 8	18	Harrison's Fourth Marine Chronometer, 1759 Winner of the Admiralty's £20,000 reward *By courtesy of the National Maritime Museum, Greenwich*	42
Watch Showing the Signs of the Zodiac, Moon Phases and Date Shagreen case with gilt metal mounts Benjamin Hill, d. 1670 *By courtesy of the Trustees of the British Museum*	20	Movement of Thomas Mudge's Timekeeper Engraving from *A Description with Plates of the Timekeeper Invented by Mr. Thomas Mudge*, 1799	43
Large Silver Watch Inscribed 'Pro F.B. M.D.' James Markwick of London, 1720 *By courtesy of the Trustees of the British Museum*	21		
Verge Watch Movements, c. 1700 Quare, Fromanteel and Clarke *By courtesy of the Director of the Science Museum*	22	Verge Watch Movements, c. 1700 Mudge, Rogers and Weston *By courtesy of the Director of the Science Museum*	44
Brass Table Clock Daniel Quare, 1648–1724 *By courtesy of the Trustees of the British Museum*	23	Harrison's First Marine Timekeeper Constructed 1729–1735 *By courtesy of the National Maritime Museum, Greenwich*	45
Engraved Dial of a Striking Clock Edward East, 1610–1673 *By courtesy of the Author*	24	Turret Clock Movement from St. Giles's Church, Cambridge Originally designed for King's College, Cambridge, by William Clement, 1671 *By courtesy of the Director of the Science Museum*	46
Brass Lantern Clock John Hilderson, c. 1665 *By courtesy of the Author*	25		
Movement of a Verge Striking Clock Design engraved by J. Mynde from W. Derham's *Artificial Clockmaker*, 1696	27	John Hilderson's Signature Engraved on the lantern clock illustrated on page 25	48

RYE CHURCH CLOCK, 1515
Dial and Quarter-Boys

PAST PRESENT AND FUTURE

For our Time is a very shadow that passeth away.

Quotation from the Book of Wisdom, 11, v.

WITH characteristic doggedness, British clock craftsmen for 350 years have striven to perfect that curious instrument the clock which measures something that does not exist: Time.

Past, present and future are intangible, but from the dawn of mankind the space of a man's day has been measured by the rising and setting of the sun. As the solar system cannot be carried around in the pocket, the early clockmaker devised the sand hour-glass and the clepsydrae (water-clocks) to measure the ebbing of time by the dripping away of water; then the "escapement" of some mechanical spring- or weight-driven machine was used to allow the mechanism to "escape" in synchronism with the setting of the sun, so to mark the hours. But what are the hours? Only since the fourteenth century has man divided the day and night into a total of twenty-four hours and in some parts of the globe they divided periods of night and day into a number of "temporal" hours, usually twelve. Often the length of an hour in the daytime was not the same as that of an hour at night, and both varied according to the seasons. In Japan temporal hours were the measure until 1870, and I treasure an old Japanese clock, the wheels of which are hand-filed out of solid steel discs, with a complicated system of weights necessitating a visit of the local Temple priests to the household every day to reset the mechanism for the appropriate temporal hours of the season.

Of course we were wise to abolish the temporal hours, but until we can devise something better than the relative and intangible Time, we can hardly hope for complete sanity! Even *Punch* on "Time" says: "The public . . . must treat Time as the fourth dimension—and like it. The boundary between past and present is not easy to define, human nature being inclined, for example, to classify a three-months-old unanswered letter as the 'present' and a day-old newspaper as the 'past'. . . ."

And when we tinker with Time and put the clocks to B.S.T., offering up a prayer, perhaps, that no longer do we have to run our days according to *D*.B.S.T., the foolishness of Time as a tape-measure of Eternity or of our lives (whichever may be the more important) is exposed by Sir Alan Herbert's jibe:

> Advance your clocks, good Briton. You will not change your ways
> Because the season changes, likewise the length of days.
> Advance your clocks, good Briton. You make me pretty sick:
> You will not get up earlier unless we play a trick.
> Advance your clocks, poor Briton: but sadly recognise—
> Here in the citadel of Truth, Big Ben is telling lies.

This peculiar non-existent and therefore intangible non-element Time is, however, the subject of our narrative, and the perfection of the measurement of this Time, which has no place in the domain of reality, has been the goal of a craft pilgrimage for British clockmakers.

I have said that they set out along this road towards the precise measurement of Time some 350 years ago, but the weight-driven clock, the use of which had spread across Europe from Italy in the very beginning of the fourteenth century, arrived in this country in about 1368, and that is truly where our British story must begin—not only the story of the Clock, but of the makers of such "orleges," "horyloges" or "horologues." Such delightful vague terminology arises from the Latin word *horologium,* and in the earliest records it is quite impossible to tell if our craftsmen in monasteries were makers of hour-glasses, water-clocks, sun-dials, horacudii (i.e. hour-striking clocks, without dials), or true timepieces bearing even the slightest resemblance to the clocks of to-day.

THIRTY-HOUR STRIKING AND ALARUM BRASS LANTERN CLOCK
Jeffrey Bayley. Signed and dated 1653

THIRTY-HOUR STRIKING HANGING CLOCK IN INLAID MARQUETERIE CASE
Christopher Gould, c. 1690

> Wel sikerer was his crowyng in his logge,
> Than is a clokke, or an abbey orlogge

wrote Chaucer in 1386, and some thirty years later Caxton printed:

> And by this tyme the Horologue had fully performed
> half his nytes cours . . .

In the year 1449 Reginald Pecock, Bishop of Chichester, proclaimed "that men schulde make and use clockis forto knowe the houris of the dai and nyt," and since then the "abbey orlogges," the clepsydrae and clock chimes of the church, the castle, the manor house, the palace, and the home, have marked Britain with a pattern of Time, until to-day the chimes of Big Ben are broadcast on short waves around the globe as a sort of horological theme-song from the heart of the Empire.

Primitive and early medieval English clocks have made former castle, abbey and manor houses live in history long after their glory would otherwise have passed away. Dover Castle, Glastonbury Abbey, the Cathedrals at Exeter, Norwich, and Peterborough: these and many others have connections with horology which in some cases transcend their importance in the busy world of to-day, and such important things as a thriving clock industry or a fine new standard of British craftsmanship have risen from the fact that in medieval monasteries it was the sacristan's duty to adjust the "orloge" to strike at the hour and awake the monks for matins. That some of these early horologes were not weight-driven clocks but merely clepsydrae is a subject antiquaries love to debate, because even the chiming clocks were worked by water, as for example the attainment of a certain level by water dripping into a basin, which would then float a ball over the rim so that it dropped on a bell: but it is interesting to turn back to Dante's *Paradiso*, which must have been written before 1321 when he died, to find in Canto X: "Then as the horologe, that calleth us, what hour the spouse of God riseth to sing her matins . . . wherein one part drawing and thrusting other, giveth a chiming sound *(tin tin sonando)* of so sweet a note . . ." And in Canto XXIV: "And even as the wheels in harmony of clock-worn so turn that the first, to whoso noteth it, seemeth still."

It seems to me that the Wicksteed translation is accurate enough to show a point of some significance, that the Italian *tin tin sonando* is imitative, and suggests a small bell of medium or high pitch, such as one associates with a chamber clock rather than the boom of an abbey bell. Machines for delivering a rapid succession of blows to a bell are depicted in many early manuscripts, and whether such mechanism was an integral part of a weight-driven clock in the fourteenth century, or whether it was separately set in motion by a clepsydra is a subject we can safely leave historians to haggle over; in any event, the critical point in the history of clocks is not the substitution of weights or spring-driven barrels for the floats of a clepsydra, but the introduction of the foliot bar or the pendulum as a mechanical "escapement" to allow the mechanical energy to "escape" away and thus enable the wheels second by second to record the passage of—of what? Shall we say of Time?

That the monks and the artificers in metal who cast the bells, built and repaired the organs and constructed the horologes were proud of their work goes without saying: that the benefits of good time-keeping were soon transferred from the cloisters to the layman's hearth, and that public clocks soon grew atop medieval religious buildings was a tribute to the ingenuity of the intricate mechanism. The very first appearance of the word "clock" (accurately, *clok*) in English literature coincides with the construction of the first public timepiece in Britain, and is in a document published in the time of Edward III, the general sense of which is: A piece of land 72 feet long and 24 feet wide in "Seynt Martynplace" in Gloucester is granted to the burghers for the erection of a tower "in which certain bells shall always sound, the hours of the day and night being indicated by a clock, vulgarly called *(clok vulgarit' nuncupata)*, placed and hung in the tower . . ."

The material used in the mechanism of such clocks was invariably iron. Most early sixteenth-century clocks, even house clocks, are of iron, but by about 1575 iron and brass were both used. Country clocks made as late as the seventeenth century are of all-iron construction, but in general it appears that the English makers and the Flemings favoured brass, while the South Germans and the Swiss prolonged what Percy Webster used to call the "Iron Age" of clocks. Apart from an initial slavish fashion in design and material, English craftsmen also at first borrowed from Continental clockmakers the diverting conceit of the automata and "jacks," or mechanical figures. It used to be held that we took the word from the French *Jacquemart*, which still survives as a French surname, derived from Jaccomarchiadus, a man in a suit of armour, but it now appears more reasonable to suppose that our stolid English "Jack" took its use from the naming of any appliance that mechanically does a man's work. We have screw-jacks, and those quaint spring- or weight-driven roasting jacks which add to the interest of the English hearth, and we even see the word verbalised so that to-day we talk of a man "jacking" up his car. Look, for instance, at *Richard II*, Act V, scene v:

> but my time
> Runs posting on in Bolingbroke's proud joy,
> While I stand fooling here, his Jack o' the clock.

What a solid English use of the word is that: and if you like to go back a little there is a 1498 reference to the history of the Church of St. Lawrence, Reading: "Item: payed for the settyng of Jak with the hangyng of his bell and mendyng his hond, iiij *d*." Not an expensive repair.

INTERIOR DIAL OF WELLS CATHEDRAL CLOCK SHOWING JOUSTING KNIGHTS
Originally made before 1394 but frequently restored

But the first British clock-tenders, clockmakers and clock-devisers were not well paid for their work. Ten shillings a year, for example, was the stipend of the "clock custodian" (but it may have been a water-clock) at Wells Cathedral in the 1400's: the exact wording of the Chapter Rolls is: *"Item: in stipendium custodientis la clokk x.s per annum."* Ten shillings a year: and they say we have avoided financial inflation. But it was not intended that the clock-tenders should go hungry. There is some thought for human needs in the Exeter Records of 1318, by which the Bishop Peter Quivil provides grants to \the bell-founder Roger de Ropford, Agnes his wife, and his son Walter: ". . . and the said Roger, Agnes and Walter and their heirs shall . . . as often as need be repair or cause to be repaired the musical instruments *(organa)* and clock *(orologium)*: while so employed all necessaries of food and drink shall be supplied to them."

Mechanical jacks on clocks never became truly anglicised, and after a time this foreign fashion was dropped. But we are left with the 4 ft. 7 in. high quarter-boys on the north face of the tower of Rye Church, with "Jack-Smite-the-Clock" at Southwold, the Blythburgh Man, the quaint little seventeenth-century jacks at Norwich, the giants atop the Thomas Harris clock in Fleet Street, London, the top-hatted man at Hagley Hall, and many similar jacks which strike the hours. Most of them do so in a way which could hardly have taxed the ingenuity of their makers, for usually the right arm alone moves, being pivoted as a simple lever at the shoulder. The figures at Southwold, Blythburgh and Wells also turn their heads, and Wells' internal popular Jack Blandifer, who sits high up on a perch inside the cathedral, has the additional accomplishment of kicking quarter-bells with his heels while using a hammer held in his hand. From Mr. Blandifer—reputed despite many coat-changes and repaintings—to be one of the earliest automata in Britain, we have a long procession of clock jacks, to the present-day Regent Street robots above Liberty's shop where St. George and the Dragon celebrate the passing of the hours thanks to the electro-mechanical apparatus, invented by F. Hope-Jones, which activates their daily tourneys to the delight of West-end shoppers.

It was during these early centuries that the craftsmanship of English workers in horology was established, but there was of course the transitional phase when timepieces were first built for other than clerical establishments, and when secular persons of exalted position were proud to possess chamber clocks ticking away their own private hours. Thus, Sir John Paston, in a letter written in the spring of 1469, says: "I praye you speke wt Harcourt off the Abbeye ffor a lytell clokke whyche I sent him . . . and as ffor mony for his labour, he hath another clok of myn whiche St. Thoms Lyndes, God have hys sowle, gave me."

Harrison Ainsworth saw the little gilt bracket clock which is said to have been given on her wedding morn to Anne Boleyn by Henry VIII, and noted that still visible on the copper-gilt weight cases were the initial letters of Henry and Anne with true lovers' knots above and below, and engraved "Dieu et mon droit . . . the most happye." "This love token of enduring affection remains the same after three centuries," commented Ainsworth, "but four years after it was given, the object of Henry's eternal love was

NICOLAUS KRATZER, ASTRONOMER TO HENRY VIII
Oil-painting by Hans Holbein, 1528

sacrificed on the scaffold. The clock still goes. It should have stopped for ever when Anne Boleyn died."

Far from stopping, the clock lived on, gathering more interesting historical associations from century to century. Horace Walpole eventually bought it, and because it "looked Gothic" he kept it in his sham collection at

WATCH IN CASE AND COVER OF SMOKE CRYSTAL WITHOUT FRAMES
AND WITH DIAL OF ENAMELLED GOLD
Michael Nouwen of London, 1609

Strawberry Hill, whence Queen Victoria bought it at the sale for just over £110. In the sale catalogue it was described in flowery auctionese as "a clock of silver, gilt, richly chased, engraved and ornamented with fleurs-de-lis," but this is pardonable salesmanship for the clock case is gilt on copper, and the weights are of lead cased in copper and gilt; the whole construction is such that South German influence is apparent though the actual workmanship may be London. In a Royal Household Book dated 1542 it appears that Henry had several such clocks: "Item: oone Clocke of iron with a case of glasse . . . Item: oone Clocke of copper and gilt, with a chyme to the same . . . Item: oone Clock of Iron with a Larum [*i.e. alarm*] to same. . . ." Henry was a pioneer among English chamber clock owners, as he was indeed a pioneer among other less praiseworthy fashions. I doubt if many of these clocks are of English manufacture. In the Privy Purse expenses of Henry VIII it is recorded that in July 1530 was paid "to a Frenchman called Drulardy for iij dyalls and a clokk for the King's Grace the sum of 15£." One Vincent Keney also received £19 16s. 8d. from the King "for xj clocks and dialls" in 1530: but it would be rash to

STRIKING CLOCK IN ENGRAVED SILVER-GILT CASE
Bartholomew Newsam, c. 1590

assume from this one record that Keney was the first English maker of chamber clocks for private use. Indeed I am forced to the conclusion that the first two English makers of such clocks who merit real attention, and whose work is extant to-day, are Bartholomew Newsam and N. Vallin who later became clockmaker to Queen Elizabeth.

Newsam appears to have been a master of his craft, and although some of his work, including one fine specimen in the British Museum, has a German flavour, he was the first of the English master makers of chamber clocks. That his work was at first influenced by European taste is not surprising, for he must have learned his craft at the hand of Kratzer, a Bavarian who resided for many years, it is said, at the Court of Henry VIII without being able to speak English, and of whom a letter was written to Cardinal Wolsey: "In these parts I met with a servant of the King's called Nicholas Craczer, a German, deviser of the King's horologues. . . ." But Newsam, before he died in 1593, created a new art form in the domestic clock, and his table clocks are a present-day delight to the eye. It was a Continental fashion to have platter-like clocks, their dials parallel with the table, and Newsam took the conventional table-clock design and gave it an English air. His work was appreciated in his day, and after a brief appointment to the Court of Queen Elizabeth he wrote petitioning Sir Philip Sidney to speak on his behalf. The petition was granted, and Newsam was granted the office of clockmaker to the Queen, for a period of three years until his death.

The evidence on N. Vallin is slender. There is a reference to one "N.V." in the Calendar of State Papers in the time of Queen Elizabeth, but this is more probably a reference to Nicholas Urseau, former clock-keeper and colleague of Kratzer "the Astronomer." In a private collection to-day, however, is a fine Elizabethan chiming clock with a carillon of thirteen bells, all of iron and brass, and beautifully fashioned, engraved at the base N. VALLIN, 1598. The clock is so far ahead of what used to be considered the technique of the late 1500's that some doubt had been thrown upon it, but now the discovery of a contemporary early English watch also signed "N. Vallin" appears to have removed all doubt. This Vallin chamber clock is of "lantern" construction, but being designed before the introduction of the oscillating pendulum the "escape" of the seconds is effected by the ticking backwards and forwards of a large balance wheel, in similar fashion to the 'scape wheel of a modern watch except of course for the absence of a "hair" spring. The balance wheel of the Vallin chamber clock is about five inches in diameter, and so heavy that it swings in its partial revolution once in two seconds.

Naturally people of refinement, or at least of wealth, were not content to leave the Time at home when they walked abroad, and it was not long before British pocket "horologes" were being made for those who could afford them. The average price of a British watch in the year 1600 was

EARLY LONG-CASE CLOCKS

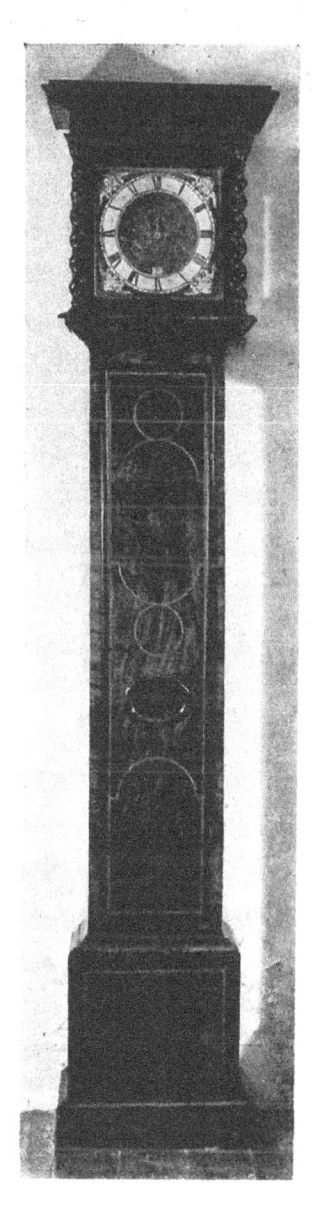

Thirty-hour, ten-inch dial clock. Walnut veneer and inlaid boxwood stringing
Thomas Tompion, c. 1675

Second-and-a-quarter clock in inlaid marqueterie case
Thomas Harris, c. 1690

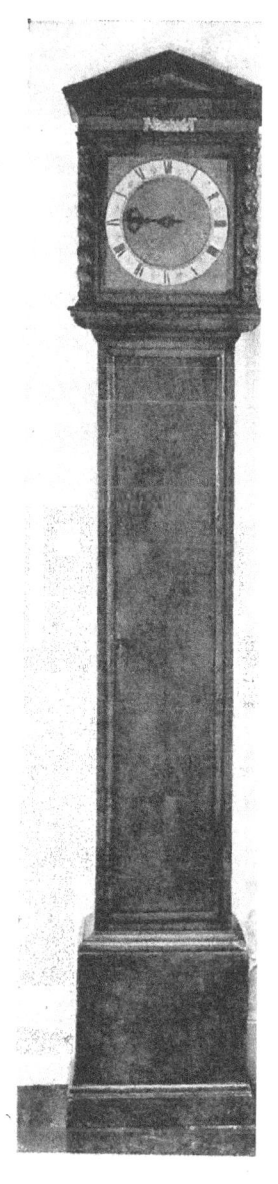

Thirty-hour, portico-top clock walnut case
Henry Crump, c. 1670

EARLY LONG-CASE CLOCKS

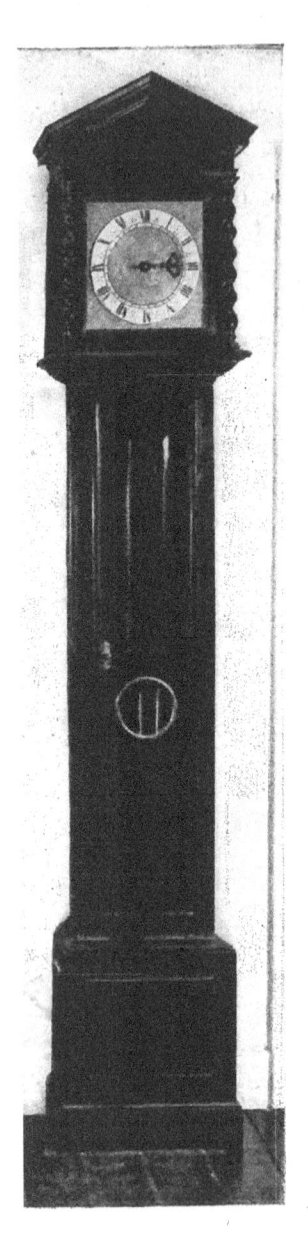

Thirty-hour striking clock with single hand and engraved dial plate. Ebony veneer on oak case
Early Daniel Quare, *c.* 1671

Ten-inch dial, striking and alarum clock in marqueterie case
Joseph Windmills, *c.* 1685

Long-case clock with skeleton silvered hour-ring cut away to show gilt dial. Walnut veneered case.
John Ebsworth, *c.* 1690

£20, which no doubt it would be fair to compare with £500 to-day. I have used the adjective "British" here advisedly, for one of this island nation's earliest watchmakers of particular renown was a Scot, David Ramsay. This Scot comes into the story in the way that Bonnie Prince Charlie came back into British history — from France. In the *Dictionary of National Biography* David Ramsay is listed as belonging to the Ramsays of Dalhousie, and David's son William recorded that "when James I succeeded to the Crown of England he sent into France for my Father, who was there, and made him page of the bedchamber and Keeper of his Majesty's Clocks and Watches." In 1622 David Ramsey [sic] is named as King's Clockmaker, and he was paid the then considerable sum of £232 15s. for repairing clocks at Theobalds and Westminster, and for making a chime of bells for a clock at Theobalds. His patron died three years later, but Ramsay kept his Court post, and there are many references in the State Papers of Charles I to Ramsay either by name, or as Page of the Bedchamber. On the 13th July 1628, for example, a warrant was signed to pay him £415 for clocks delivered for the king's service. His early work is beautiful, and bears many signs of a distinct break-away from the South German tradition. The British Museum collection of watches includes a gold watch by Ramsay, the period being about 1600, and it is signed "David Ramsay, Scotus, me fecit." Such treasures were often mislaid for many generations, and within living memory the tapestry which had decorated the dining-room of Gawdy Hall was taken down for preservation, and in the wall mouldings behind the tapestry was found a small star-shaped watch, together with some silver apostle spoons and documents bearing silent witness to the dangerous days of Cromwell. The silver watch was made by Ramsay, and it may well have been one of the little pocket watches included in the trio which he made in the year 1612, when, so the records of the Keeper of the Privy Purse show, there were: "Watches, three, bought of Mr. Ramsay the Clockmaker lx li" (i.e. £60), and they are listed among the King's "Guyftes and Rewardes," so that one may well have found its way to the former owners of Gawdy Hall.

In *The Fortunes of Nigel* you will find that Scott introduces Ramsay as the keeper of a shop a few yards east of Temple Bar, and in a note to "Nigel," Ramsay is described as "Constructor of Horologes to his Most Sacred Majesty James I." It is strange that Scott should parade such a pedantic word as "horologe," for by now the word "clock" had even become common as an English surname, one of the most interesting curiosities of horology, surely. Even in Ramsay's time we find a reference in State Papers to one John Clock, of Staple Inn, Middlesex, who is to receive £20 lent by him to the King on Privy seal: and there is in 1618 a reference to one Petter [sic] Clocke, living in St. Olave's, Southwark.

Although the Dutch word *clok* had grown thus into common usage, British craftsmen were not a little concerned about the influx of foreign workmen to London, particularly, and very early in the seventeenth century there were fifteen clockmakers and two watchmakers in London, all of whom were foreigners. By *A true Certificat of the Names of the Straungers residing and dwellinge within the City of London* taken by the Privy Council in 1618, we find that in the ward of Farringdon Within was then living "Barnaby Martinot, clock-maker, born in Paris, a Roman Catholique." And in Portsoken Ward was living "John Goddard, clockmaker; lodger and servant with Isack Sunes in Houndsditch; born at Paris, Fraunce; heer 3 yeers; a papist; yet he hath taken the oath of allegiance to the king's supremacy, and doth acknowledg the king for his soveraigne dureing his abode in England."

The fact that these foreign workmen were willing, though "Catholiques," "papists," and "of the Romish church," to give an oath of allegiance to the king, so that they might peacefully ply their trade in the City of London, was a serious thorn in the side of the British craftsmen, who no doubt felt that the nation had little use now for foreign workmen or their ideas, and that the quality of the British work justified some State protection against this invasion. In the spring of 1622 a petition was drawn up complaining to the king of the "great number and deceitful tricks" of foreigners practising their trade, and begging that they might not be permitted to work except under English masters, and that no foreign clocks might be imported. A crisis had been reached in this early phase of the history of British clockmaking. Obviously something had to be done, and by a curious stroke it was the Scot, David Ramsay, who did it.

JEFFREY BAYLEY'S SIGNATURE

THE WORSHIPFUL COMPANY

One can buy ordinary watches in London at three guineas in silver, and seven in gold, and upwards. Precision timekeepers are nowhere better or more perfectly made than in London . . .

Philipp Andreas Nemmich's account of a Journey to Britain, 1806

NOT all the glory of triumph in the sphere of Time measurement is due to the clockmakers. The men whose work inspires these pages almost preclude the idea of death, but their genius in fashioning things with their hands, in filing beautiful clock parts from drawn steel and cast brass was aided by the skill and ingenuity of many leaders of scientific thought and learning. The Worshipful Company of British Clockmakers was helped beyond all measure by Robert Hooke, by Sir Christopher Wren, by Flamstead, William Derham, and even by Sir Isaac Newton, who when lodging in an apothecary's house in Grantham, at the age of twelve, built himself a water clock.

Although we talk to-day of clockmaking as an art, or as the progression towards precision timekeeping of almost fantastic exactitude, according to the branch of horological appreciation which we feel most deeply, the blunt truth is that with very few exceptions clockmaking for over 500 years has been a business, and not a dilettante devotion. Clockmakers are businessmen, in trade, and the only ideas they were able to absorb from the Hookes and the Isaac Newtons were those which would facilitate construction (very important in the era when it took months to make and assemble a clock), or make their timekeepers more accurate than those of their competitors.

So it was that the quarrel with the invading foreign workmen in the City of London assumed proportions which, though unfortunately common to-day, were of vital importance to the early seventeenth-century craftsmen who had their apprentices to pay and their families to keep. The petition of 1622 had set the ball rolling. Five years later there was a proposal put forward, no doubt, by some French members of the Court who wanted a more plentiful supply of watches and trinkets, to grant letters patent to French clockmakers to carry on their trade in London. It was this which really took the London craftsmen by the ears. Before then, individual craftsmen had usually kept their status by being associated with one or other of the existing Companies—the Blacksmiths' as a rule. But the French competition forced their hand, and in 1630 they went into conclave, drawing up a petition as a result of which the new Clockmakers' Company came into being, in August, 1631.

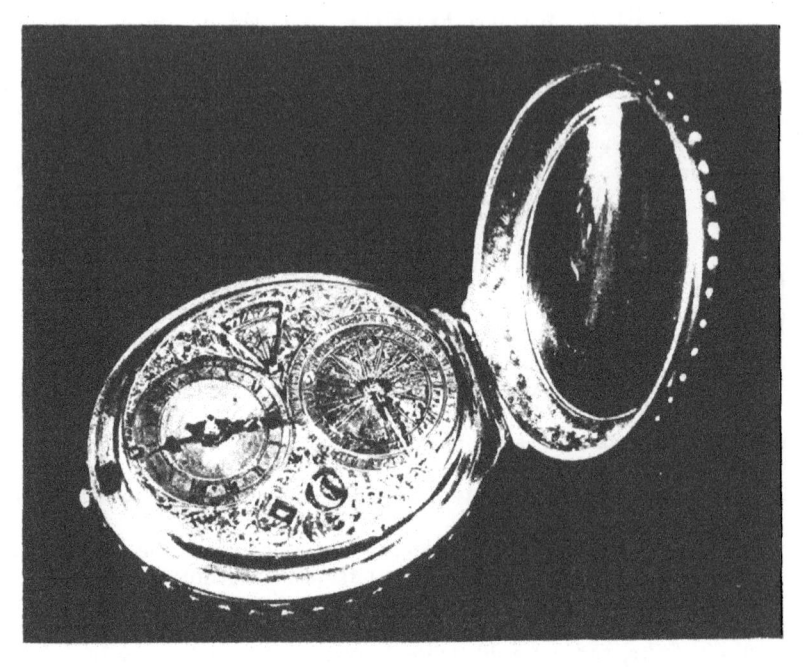

WATCH SHOWING THE SIGNS OF THE ZODIAC, MOON-PHASES AND DATE
Benjamin Hill, d. 1670

The Worshipful Company was incorporated by Royal Charter from Charles I as "The Master, Wardens and Fellowship of the Art of Clockmakers of the City of London." The company had power by their charter to make by-laws for the government of all craftsmen using the trade in London, or within a radius of ten miles, and for the regulation in general terms of the way in which the trade should be carried out *throughout the realm.*

Although the jurisdiction of the Clockmakers' Company was limited to the capital, the influence was very strong and spread more specially to Edinburgh, where the craft also very soon arrived at a high standard.

To prevent the public from being injured by persons "making, buying, selling, transporting and importing any bad, deceitful or insufficient clocks, watches, larums, sundials, boxes or cases for the said trade," powers were given to the Company by charter "to enter with a constable or other officer, any ships, vessels, warehouses, shops, or other places, where they shall suspect such bad and deceitful works to be made or kept, for the purpose of searching for them," and if entrance should be denied they might effect

LARGE SILVER WATCH INSCRIBED 'PRO F.B. M.D.'
James Markwick of London, 1720

it by force. The right of entry was constantly exercised until the end of the century. The town was divided into districts, periodic searches were made and many instances are recorded of deceitful works being found and broken up, or of masters taking on too many apprentices so that there would be a danger of "mass-production," and of a consequent reduction in quality standards.

The Scot, Ramsay, was elected first Master, and Henry Archer, John Wellowe and Sampson Shelton were the first wardens. The Company from their establishment in 1631, having no hall, held their meetings at some tavern in the City. In 1656, the famous clockmaker, Ahasuerus Fromanteel, and some thirty other members were forced to complain at this lack of dignity.

Many other famous Companies had their City halls, and many other Companies had also tried hard for livery and succeeded. The Clockmakers' Company had no hall, no livery. Fromanteel, who was in fact to engage himself in fairly constant bickering with the officials of the Company for many years, registered a complaint that "in spite of members having to pay 4d. a quarter, the Companye's meetings are still held in Taverns." Fromanteel, of Dutch extraction, may have had therefore a personal reason for differing in many ways from the Company's rulings, and he also became restive under the somewhat inquisitorial proceedings of the Company's court of inquiry about his large number of apprentices and their antecedents. But any pressure which he put on the elders of the Company to build a hall fitting to the craft was unfortunately counteracted by the Fire. The Castle Tavern in Fleet Street, where the meetings were so often held, was afterwards rebuilt, and under the ownership of Sir John Tash, an Alderman of the City and a wealthy wine-merchant, it became for some years the home once again of the clockmakers. In 1671 the Company was granted the honour of carrying arms, and in view of the considerable number of women workers as silversmiths it is interesting to note that so early in the history of the Clockmakers' Company as 1715, sanction was given to female apprentices. For many years the Company petitioned for livery, but this was not granted until 1767, some fifty years after the death of most of the famous early craftsmen whose names appear in this present volume: and incidentally it is to be noted that although the Clockmakers are an integral part of the grand guild system which has helped to make British workmanship what it is to-day, quite a number of clockmakers (such as John and Joseph Knibb) must have envinced hostility to the, at times, autocratic methods of the Company, and never submitted themselves for Mastership. Even the great Thomas Tompion, buried in Westminster Abbey and recognised to-day as the Father of English clockmaking, was admitted a freeman by redemption in 1674, and served thirty years before deigning to accept the Mastership.

The granting of livery was a turning-point in the recognition of clockmaking as a true craft

VERGE WATCH MOVEMENTS
c. 1700
Quare, Fromanteel, and Clarke

BRASS TABLE CLOCK
Daniel Quare, 1648–1724

among the fine arts, and on the inauguration of Thomas Harley, brother of the Earl of Oxford, on Lord Mayor's Day, 9th November, 1767, a London news-letter records: "The Tin-Plate Workers' Company and the Clockmakers' Company joined the Lord Mayor's procession for the first time since they were made Livery-Companies, and made a genteel appearance."

Now it would be a pleasant tribute to the history of British clock and watchmaking if the stories could be told of all the important, interesting, inventive and creative craftsmen of this gallant Company, from its inception

ENGRAVED DIAL OF A STRIKING CLOCK
Edward East, 1610–1673

in 1631 to the present day. But unfortunately there are considerable gaps in the chronicles, partly through failure to keep records, partly through the change in clockmaking from craftsmanship to mass-production (an important source of omission, this, for the research of present-day collectors stops short at a period long before the Swiss clock and the American watch), and partly through the splitting up of the interests and energies of the old clockmakers themselves to other guilds and learned societies.

We may learn much more of George Graham, for instance, from the Proceedings of the Royal Society, of which he was a distinguished member, than from the minutes of the Clockmakers' Company: yet Graham was Tompion's companion and successor, and to-day they lie together in Westminster.

BRASS LANTERN CLOCK
John Hilderson, *c.* 1665

The biographical facts about the pioneer clockmakers can be seen in many works of reference, notably the late F. J. Britten's *Old Clocks and Watches*, which gives a list of some 12,000 makers. There is a short bibliography of other works at the end of this volume, and I acknowledge credit to nearly all of them for extracts given here—but especially to Britten's, which is the vade-mecum. *Who* they were is not nearly so important as *where* they were, and how they worked: and to those in search of a hobby I suggest the tracking-down of places of business of the clockmakers, and investigation of their early shops, forges and stock-rooms. In the country you may pleasurably search parish records and even advertise, as I have done, in county papers for family-trees and other documents about the makers. And in the City of London you can tread the ground where many famous clock-shops once stood, and where Edward East sold watches to Charles I, from his lodgings and clock-premises in Fleet Street; or where Henry Jones, East's apprentice, sold "ye first barometers whiche were yet made in England," from his shop by the Inner Temple Gate.

It can be a fascinating study, for although from 1660 to 1780 the "great" makers worked all within about five square miles, with the Royal Exchange as the focal point, their exact place of business was seldom given. Even as late, comparatively, as 1789, Thomas Earnshaw, one of the inventors of the chronometer, was told by Dr. Maskelyne, the Astronomer Royal, that an order for two marine watches had been lost to Earnshaw, because Maskelyne did not know where he worked. From my own collection of antique English clocks I have discovered that the maker often gave his place of business for the first few years, but later was content with the bold "London" or *Londini fecit* (made in London), leaving it to his patrons to say: "I bought my fob watch from Charles Gretton, over against Sergeants Inn Gate," or "My fine new gilt brass clock came from Richard Ames, near St. Andrews Church in Holborn." I have one of the first long-case clocks ever made by Daniel Quare, the great Quaker clock craftsman second in importance only to Tompion. That clock is signed *Daniel Quare in Martins Le Grand Londini fecit*, but many years before Quare became famous and made clocks for William III (you can see his handiwork to-day in Hampton Court) he was content to give his address merely as "London," though in fact he had moved to The King's Arms, Exchange Alley—near where the statue of Rowland Hill now stands. Even when the name and address were given, changes in geography or errors in engraving make it difficult to identify them. Thus John Hilderson's early clocks were signed "in Chessil-street," a thoroughfare which I have failed to find on the old London maps, and a Joseph Saer clock (*circa* 1687) in my collection, as well as a few others, are signed "Joseph Saer in purpoole Lane, Londini," which is a mis-engraving either for Penpoole or Purple. We may never know which.

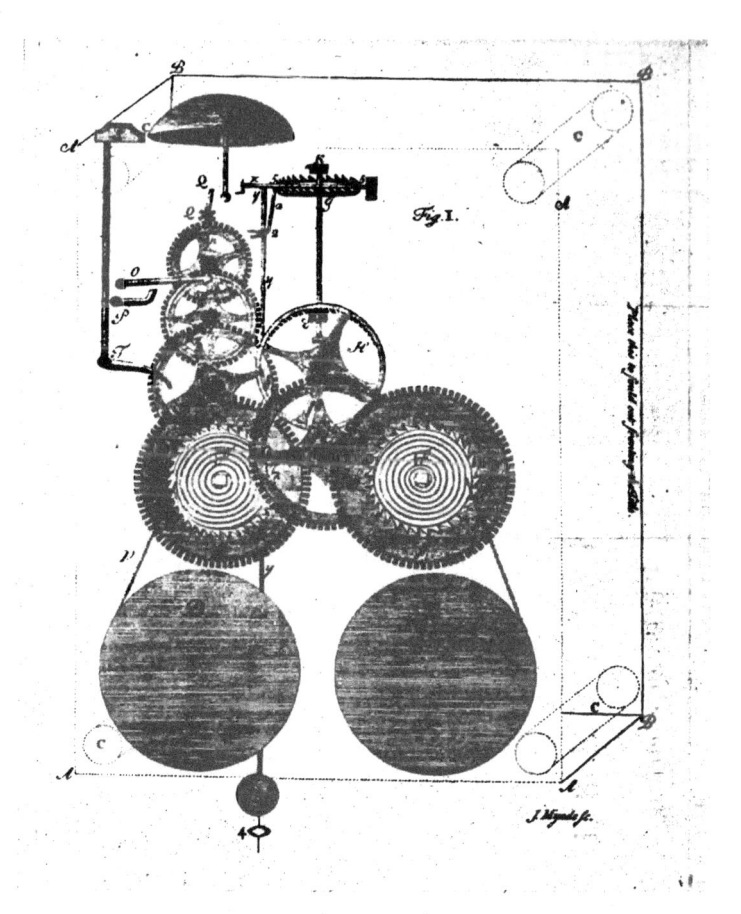

MOVEMENT OF A VERGE STRIKING CLOCK
Design engraved by J. Mynde from William Derham's *Artificial Clockmaker*, 1696

Sweeting's Alley, probably a corruption of Swithin's, was near Cornhill and the Royal Exchange, and for some hundred years was a favourite spot with the craft, but it perished in 1838 when the old Exchange buildings were destroyed by fire. Fleet Street, home of many fine clockmakers, remains unchanged, and the little turning off it, Water Lane (the scene of so much of Tompion's work) is now Whitefriars Street. Glass for the bezels and lenticles of many old seventeenth-century London clocks was made at the Whitefriars glassworks between this street and the Thames—

a glass foundry mentioned by Pepys and still producing British glass today, though on another site.

There are, as I have said, inevitable gaps in the chronicles of the clock craftsmen, and it would be too much to expect the story of some 300 years of quest for precision time-keeping to be told without some omissions in the telling. But as Robert Gould says in his *Antiquities of Freemasonry,* "Between the region of fancy and the province of authenticated history lies a borderland of tradition, full of difficulties which can neither be passed without notice nor ever perhaps finally explained. . . ." If we cannot always have authenticated history we will at least keep away from the region of fancy! The tales I tell here are culled from that amusing *Artificial Clockmaker,* first published in 1696 by William Derham, D.D., a Divine who came up from Worcester to become not only Canon of Windsor, but a recognised authority among clockmaking technicians ("Artificial," of course, is explained by the complete change of meaning of the word in the eighteenth century: in the preceding century the accent was on the "art"); from the Diary of Robert Hooke, the wild-eyed genius who was colleague and friend of Sir Christopher Wren, Sir Jonas Moore and Tompion; from old publications, broad-sheets and news-letters including *The London Gazette,* John Smith's *Horological Dialogues* of 1675, *The Commonwealth Mercury, The Affairs of the World* (1700), *A Pacquet from Wells* (1701), *The Daily Post, The Daily Advertiser,* the *London Magazine,* and from many similar records which combine to give a photographic impression of the rich, industrious life of the old makers. Some, like Tompion and Quare, were honoured to become Court clockmakers. Some, like Edmund Denison Beckett, designer of the movement of Big Ben's clock, were raised to the Peerage (he became Baron Grimthorpe), and some, like Christopher Gould, died bankrupt; just before he died, a petition was raised that he might be given the post of ale-taster, to save him from the debtors' prison. Of such varied stuff are the clockmakers made.

Edward East, first of the famous company of clockmakers after Newsam and Ramsay, has one of the most famous names in English horology, but the present evidence shows that there must have been two Edward Easts, probably father and son. An Edward East was established in Fleet Street in 1635. Lady Fanshawe tells in her memoirs how, when she came from France, she was sent to lodge with Mr. East the Watchmaker in 'Fleete Streete'. Before that he must have had watchmaking premises near the Mall, and his early silver-dial watches were given by the King as presents in seventeenth-century tennis tournaments. One of East's watches was always kept at the bedside of Charles I, who is said to have wound it himself and taken great pride in its alarm mechanism. The watch woke the King up on 30th January, 1649, the morning of his execution, and was given by Charles on the way to the scaffold to a courtier, Sir Thomas

Herbert, and for 200 years it stayed in the Herbert family.

Even thirty years after Charles's death, another Edward East was still famous as a clock and watchmaker. The son, if son it be, has left us many fine long-case clocks, the later specimens of which were made at "Ye Sun, outside Temple Bar," but most East workmanship is signed in the Latin fashion, "Eduardus East, Londini."

It is worth digressing here from chronological order to another famous maker, Henry Jones, for he was an apprentice of the East family. He tramped to London from Southampton and served his apprenticeship with East from the age of twenty-two. We have North's *Life* as evidence that "barometers were first made and sold by one Jones, a noted clockmaker, in the Inner Temple Gate, at the instance of Lord Keeper Guildford." That Jones also made many pocket watches is proved—as in the case of several other famous makers—by the considerable number of "Lost and Wanted" advertisements we find in the old records: yet to-day a Henry Jones watch is a comparative rarity, and we know him chiefly by his clocks. A typical advertisement is in the *London Gazette* for October, 1689, and reads: "Lost on the 21st Instant, between the Hay Market near Charing

TAVERN CLOCK IN TRUNK CASE, *c.* 1760
Mahogany case with applied decoration carved and gilded

Cross and the Rummer in Queen Street, a round gold Pendulum Watch . . . it was made by one Henry Jones, Watchmaker in The Temple, the Out case had a Cypher pin'd on It, and the Shagreen much worn. . . ." Jones crops up in history again when he made the clock which Charles II gave to Mrs. Jane Lane in memory of her services after the Battle of Worcester.

A colleague of the Easts was John Hilderson, one of the several early makers who for some 300 years have remained almost in obscurity and who are historically speaking only now being discovered. The few clocks signed by him are of the same high quality as East's early work, and his zenith appears to be in the 1660–65 era. There is a Dutch tang about the name, and at least three of his clocks are strongly reminiscent of the Dutch craftsmanship which came to Britain during the early part of the seventeenth century, and which was soon absorbed by the better quality of the English work, transformed in the course of the quest for precision timekeeping, but which still kept its distinctive art form and, so some like to believe to-day, began a horological tradition.

HOOD OF LONG-CASE CLOCK WITH LACQUERED DECORATION
James Markwick, c. 1720

But is this tradition Dutch any more than the Classic style of Wren is Dutch merely because Wren's best work was produced at a time when the Orange influence on London and society was at its height? The rise of the City merchants, the growth of the nation's total population to something like five millions, and the gradual establishment of a prosperous middle class, with the decline in the power of the Crown, meant that many thousands of potential purchasers awaited the trinkets, watches and proud household timepieces which the brethren of the Clockmakers' Company could produce. And of course they wanted these things in a style enabling them to ape their betters. The successful clothier could not bring a Wren cornice or architrave to every feature of his grand new town house, but he did like to see these Classic details reproduced in his furniture, and especially in his costly pieces, such as clocks. The prosperous wine merchant had, in the course of his trade, helped in the reaction against Puritanism, but nevertheless he did not think it odd that his clock cases should be in the Puritan style, ebony veneered on oak, of the type extensively made in Holland and England, but now labelled Dutch. Indeed the case-makers set a convention which was slow to change. As late as 1675 Sir Richard Legh (according to a record discovered by the horologist John James, and published in *The Antique Collector*) went to buy a new clock. "I went to the famous pendulum maker Knibb," he wrote, "and have agreed for one, he having none ready but one dull stager which was at £19. For £5 more I have agreed for one finer than my father's, and it is to be better finished with carved capitals gold, and gold pedistals with figures of boys and cherubims all brass gilt. I would have had it olivewood (the case I mean) but gold does not agree with the colour, so took their advice to have it black ebony which suits your cabinet better than walnut-tree wood, of which they are mostly made...."

In clock design the so-called Dutch tradition includes mantel clocks with ebony veneer, a portico top supported on pillars in the beam-and-lintel fashion, a narrow hour ring, a spade hour hand. But the use of the Classic Orders has run through British architecture and British furniture since the days of Inigo Jones, when the Palladian style, named after the Italian architect Palladio, became the vogue, and the classic elements of the plinth, column and portico were worked willy-nilly into building and furnishing. If any proof were needed that the use of the Classic style in English clocks is not predominantly a Dutch characteristic, it is to be found, I think, in the excellence of the British workmanship and the stern adherence to Classic rules. The capitals of Ionic and Corinthian columns used in the casework of early Quare, Knibb, East, Hilderson and Henry Jones clocks were finely finished, and—more important—in the English clock case the proportions of the architrave and portico are strictly derived, as they should be, from the diameter of the column. The Dutch case-makers, in clocks earlier and later than the English, did not follow this strict Classic tradition, and to our eye the cases appear ill-proportioned, with the architrave and frieze too top-heavy for the columns. Oddly enough, when the Classic revival came in Victorian days, and portico-and-pillar marble clocks were mass-produced in their thousands, it was the Dutch fashion which was followed, and not the English classic. There is evidence that Hooke, Wren and Tompion were in consultation, and that Tompion's grandest cases were strictly architectural. Even when Tompion designed a special clock for his friend "Beau" Nash, for the new Pump Room at Bath, completed 1706, he used a strongly architectural motif of a Doric column to harmonise with the column-motif of the Pump Room, and indeed the whole oak case is built behind a half-section of a column, down which the clockweight can fall, with the pendulum swinging behind. It is appropriate here to point out that our ancestors did not refer to "grandfather" clocks, but to "tall" or "long-case" or even "coffin" clocks. The so-called "bracket" clock of to-day was in its time a mantel clock. "Grandfather clock" did not inflict itself on us until some time after the 1880's, when that song "My Grandfather's Clock" swept England and America, and then of course it became something implying derision, and not a furnishing style of fashion!

It is in the era of the Fromanteels, a famous, thriving family of craftsmen who operated in London from about 1625, that the mingling of Dutch and English styles is seen to best advantage. An entry in his diary dated 1st November, 1660, from Evelyn reads: "I went with some of my relations to Court, to shew them his Ma[ties] cabinet and closset of rarities . . . amongst the clocks, one that shew'd the rising and setting of the Syn in y[e] Zodiaq, the Sunn represented by a face and rais of gold, upon an azure skie . . . rising and setting behind a landscape of hills, the work of our famous Fromantel. . . ." And on another occasion Evelyn refers to Fromanteel and "Zulichem" in one single entry, Zulichem being the district in Holland from which Christiaan Huygens originated, and the place-name being used as a surname in the fashion common in bygone times. "I return'd," he wrote, "by Fromanteel's, the famous clockmaker, to see some pendules, Monsieur Zulichem being with us." Despite the importance of the Fromanteels—Ahasuerus, Daniel, John, Abraham and their sons— and the prolificacy of their handiwork, few Fromanteel clocks have survived, so they are much sought after by collectors. A grievous loss in the bombing of the Dutch Church of Austin Friars, during London's long blitzkrieg, was the destruction of a fine long-case Fromanteel.

It seems certain that after Christiaan Huygens, Evelyn's "Monsieur Zulichem," first applied the pendulum to the timepiece, one of the Fromanteel family returned to Amsterdam to become apprenticed to one Samuel Coster, the first craftsman to construct a clock with the "Huygens" pendulum. Within six months the London Fromanteel family were advertising in *The Commonwealth Mercury* of 25th November, 1658: "There is lately

LONG-CASE CLOCKS OF THE EIGHTEENTH CENTURY

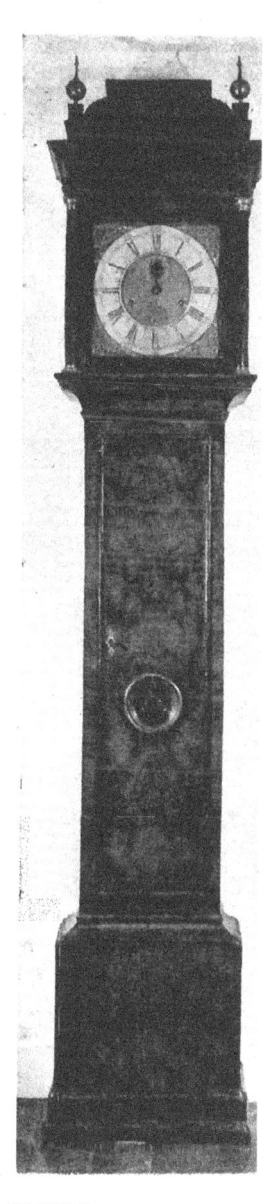

Twelve-inch arch dial clock in Mahogany case
John Ross of Tain, *c.* 1780

Early arch dial clock. Walnut case
Joseph Windmills, *c.* 1710

Twelve-inch dial month c
with semi-sonniary striking
Daniel Quare, *c.* 1720

ALARUM AND STRIKING MANTEL CLOCK IN EBONY-VENEERED CASE
Henry Jones, c. 1685

a way found out for making Clocks that go exact and keep equaller time then [sic] any now made without this Regulator (examined and approved before his Highness the Lord Protector, by such Doctors whose knowledge and learning is without exception) and are not subject to alter by change of weather as others are, and may be made to go a week, or a moneth, or a year, with once winding up, as well as those that are wound up every day, and keep time as well; and is very excellent for all House Clocks that go either with Springs or Waights: and also Steeple Clocks that are most subject to differ by change of weather. Made by Ahasuerus Fromanteel who made the first that were in ENGLAND. You may have them at his House on the Bank-side in Mosses-Alley, SOUTHWARK, and at the Sign of the Maremaid in Lothbury, near Bartholomew-Lane end, London."

Not all the fine makers began in London; some were attracted from their country workshops by the fame and fortunes to be made in London. Some, like John Knibb, couldn't bear to work there. The Knibbs were a prolific family of clockmakers, including Joseph, John, Edward, Peter and Samuel, but the two whose work remains probably most important to-day are the brothers Joseph and John. They were Oxford men and first set up business in the parish of St. Clements. At times they were at loggerheads with the guildsmen of Oxford, but in 1689 made their peace, and a year later Joseph Knibb moved to London, setting up in business it would appear at "the sign of the Dyal, near Serjeants-Inn." John remained behind, and in 1700 became Mayor of Oxford. Tiring of London life at the close of the seventeenth century, Joseph Knibb sold up his effects, after a life-time's clock and watchmaking, first at the "Dyal" and then at a more fashionable address, nearer Whitehall, in Suffolk Street, and he moved to Hanslope, a small village near Stony Stratford. He did not cease making fine clocks, however, and Knibb clocks signed "Joseph Knibb of Hanslop" are more rare to-day than those *"Londini fecit,"* and are much sought.

Public clocks by the pioneer makers have survived, though unfortunately there are now many with the hands of Esau and the works of Jacob. So early as 1630 Ahasuerus Fromanteel had been noted in the parish records of East Smithfield as a maker of steeple clocks. During the building of St. Paul's it was commonly said that Wren had asked Tompion to build a masterpiece of a clock for this masterpiece of a cathedral, and a newsletter of 1700 records that Tompion had contracted for £3,000 to erect such a clock, to run for a hundred years at one winding. Subsequently it was Langley Bradley, spoken of by Derham as "the judicious Workman of Fenchurch-street" who built the clock for Wren, and within a twelvemonth he must have had cause for regret.

St. Paul's clock, which ran until the movement was replaced by the present one in 1892, was built by Bradley for £308 9s. 10d., and the task was completed by 1708. But Bradley became involved in the disputes which involved Wren, Jennings, the chief carpenter, and the Dean himself, and so bitter were the wranglings that in 1713 a pamphlet was produced: "Fact Against Scandal: or a Collection of Testimonials, Affidavits and other Authentick Proofs in Vindication of Mr. Richard Jennings, Carpenter, Langley Bradley, Clock-Maker and Richard Phelps, Bell-Founder: To be referr'd to in an Answer which will speedily be publish'd to a late false and malicious Libel Entituled: Frauds and Abuses at St. Paul's."

From this document it appears that a minimum wage of 11s. a week was paid to the clock builders and carpenters, and that the chief retort of Bradley to those who said the clock was always wrong, and no true standard of time for the metropolis, was the meddling of people who were let into the tower to see the great bell, and who then tinkered with the works. "It is not the fault of the Clock," wrote Bradley," but by its being made a Show of." And he was probably true at that, for subsequently he built clocks for Cripplegate Church and St. Clement Danes in the Strand, and there were no complaints. In the first St. Paul's clock there was no dial, the chimes being considered sufficient for a clerical building, and a clock-face incongruous. The Church of St. Vedast, Foster Lane, so cruelly damaged in the 1941 German raids, also originally had a turret movement which struck bells but did not show the time on a dial. Bradley's clock in St. Clements was subsequently modified to strike each hour twice. The main strike of the hour was given on the great 24-hundredweight bell, and then this was echoed by the small Sanctus bell in the tower—a fifteenth-century bell said to have been used before the Reformation. This Sanctus could not be heard during the day as its faint echo of the great bell was drowned by the traffic's roar, but the Luftwaffe has silenced both.

"I will do one thing more of which London shall not show the Like," boasted Thomas Harris (or Harrys), whose premises were at the Blackfriars end of Water Lane, when Tompion's shop was at the brow of the hill leading into Fleet Street. "I will make two hands show the hours and minutes without the church (St. Dunstan's), upon a double dial, which will be worth your observation, and to my credit." Also he proposed to build a portico under which two figures of men with pole-axes would strike the quarters—all for the sum of £80, including free maintenance. The Vestry compromised, gave him £35 and the old clock, and £4 a year for keeping in order the Gog and Magog display which still amuses Fleet Street—the only jack-clock in the City. Fleet Street has long been associated with these mechanisms, for there was a jack-clock on show in 1478, and Stowe describes a conduit in that year near Shoe Lane, with angels having "sweet sounding bells before them" on which hymns were played. Tom Harris's Gog and Magog were taken away when the old church was pulled down, were sold at auction to the Marquis of Hertford for £210, and for nearly a century they worked and chimed the hours and quarters in Regent's Park. But by the generosity of Lord Northcliffe the old figures and part of the original clock were restored to St. Dunstan's—not all of it Harris's work,

HANGING CLOCK
Mahogany case with applied carved and gilt decoration, c. 1760

for in 1738 the parish spent £110 for repairs. The *Mirror* of 1828, then published from Fleet Street, complained of the rival attraction of the Fleet Street clock jacks, saying: "one would really suppose they were in league with the pickpockets," for many a passing Londoner had his pocket picked or his watch stolen while gaping up at Harris's moving figures. Two years later the clock was sold at auction to the Marquis, but one might quote the motto of the Clockmakers' Company, *Tempus Rerum Imperator*—Time the governor of all things—for now the clock is back again in Fleet Street, and the *Mirror* is published from an office in a side-thoroughfare.

While Langley Bradley, Tom Harris, Daniel Delander, Christopher Gould, Charles Gretton and many another fine maker were following in Tompion's footsteps, Tompion's own nephew and chief apprentice, "Honest George" Graham was also following in the steps of the master craftsman, and creating a new standard of horological precision and ingenuity.

Graham, a Cumberland lad who found his way to London at the age of fourteen, apprenticed to Henry Aske ("at Ye Cross Keys in Bethlem") the very next year, became not only Tompion's apprentice and disciple, but the forerunner of a line of British clock craftsmen who set out to make clocks and chronometers (a device until Graham's time not considered possible) more exact than ever before. For seventeen years he worked with Tompion at the Water Lane shop, and many of Tompion's late clocks made just prior to his death in 1713 and signed "Thos: Tompion, Londini," were probably the work of Graham. Seven years after Tompion's death Graham moved to a better shop a little nearer Fleet Bridge—premises which passed into the hands of Mudge, and subsequently Mudge's son in partnership with Dutton, and so stayed as a clock shop until about fifty years ago. Graham's trade in watches was considerable, and his inventions for watchmaking improvements were almost as revolutionary and beneficial as his discovery of the "dead-beat" escapement for precision clockwork. Yet his trade reputation in his day must have been built up more on showy goods, for the *London Magazine* of 1753 in a satire "Ingredients required for the Manufacture of a Fop" lists:

> A repeater by Graham, which the hours reveals
> Almost over-balanc'd with knick-knacks and seals.

As the years progressed, Graham devoted more of his time to the perfection of timekeeping than to immediate profits from the merely commercial run of clocks and watches, and in the same year that he took over the new shop, next the Duke of Marlborough's Head Tavern, he was elected to membership of the Royal Society. Becoming engrossed in precision work and astronomical research, he was a valued coadjutor of Halley and Bradley. His scientific inventions include the first application of the timepiece to the telescope, in the form we know to-day as the transit clock, for

DEAD-BEAT ESCAPEMENT
Model of the escapement invented by George Graham, c. 1715

keeping an equatorially-mounted telescope fixed upon a star. Indeed the first transit clock in Greenwich Observatory was Graham's handiwork. If the seconds hand of an ordinary long-case clock be watched carefully, it will be seen that the anchor mechanism of the escapement permits a slight recoil, and in addition to ticking away the seconds the hand appears to bounce slightly in even the best set-up clock. This source of error and friction could not be overcome until Graham invented the non-recoiling dead-beat escapement, which at the time appeared to be the necessary perfection for astronomical timepieces. Although the observatory clock to-day has far surpassed Graham's limits of tolerance, the dead-beat escapement is still in use, and most watchmakers have as their standard regulator a weight-driven timepiece with a dead-beat escapement. Another landmark in horology was reached by Graham in the devising of the cylinder escapement. Although at that time a Fellow of the Royal Society, and anxious to devote his major energies to pure scientific research, Graham was determined to reduce the errors in timekeeping of pocket watches brought about by the use of the simple verge escapement. The result of his researches described in several papers read before the Royal Society was the cylinder escapement, which has remained unchanged for some 220 years, and is the standard escapement now in all mass-produced pocket- and wrist-watches. The discovery was made about 1725 and in a letter to his Paris colleague, Julien Le Roy, he communicated the invention and so introduced it to France. The mercury-compensated pendulum was another Graham innovation, first given to the world a year after the cylinder-escapement discovery, and in his paper, read to the Royal Society in 1726, Graham described it as "A Contrivance to Avoid Irregularities in a Clock's Motion by the Action of Heat and Cold upon a Pendulum"—basically, the substitution of a container of mercury for the solid metal bob of a pendulum, to counteract errors caused by the expansion of the pendulum rod and associate mountings in warm weather.

Despite these high-flights into scientific research and horological improvement, Graham made many clocks and watches and a comparatively large number exists to-day. That he was a popular maker of domestic clocks is shown by the inclusion of a characteristic Graham ebony-veneer mantel clock in Hogarth's famous family portrait of the Graham Family. Thirty-eight years after the death of the Father of English Clockmaking, the Tompion grave near the western entrance of Westminster Abbey was opened to receive the body of his nephew. The inscription reads: " . . . George Graham of London, Watchmaker and F.R.S., whose Curious Inventions do honour to Y^e British Genius." Graham, Honest George from Cumberland, had achieved more than skill in craftsmanship. He had begun a new era, and shown the way to real precision in timekeeping—that precision which was soon to become vital in ensuring Britain's supremacy at sea, through accurate marine navigation.

CHRISTOPHER GOULD'S SIGNATURE

TIME IS PRECIOUS

When we consider all the achievements of science to-day and the aid we derive from them in measuring time, it becomes a matter of marvel how the old scientists and astronomers ... were able to get any degree of accuracy.

H. Alan Lloyd's *500 Years of Precision Time-keeping*, 1938

BEFORE George Graham opened up a new field in precision time-keeping with the compensated pendulum and the dead-beat escapement, the pioneer English clockmakers had resorted to a number of tricks to compensate for the errors. The Fromanteel family were among the first to use the device of a spring-loaded maintaining-power to keep the clock running during the few seconds taken by winding, when the clock might otherwise be slowed down as the weight would be taken by the hand and would not be available to drive the clock. Such an error, though small, would be cumulative in a thirty-hour or eight-day clock; so to ensure that the maintaining-power mechanism is brought into play each time the clock is wound, shutters are arranged to cover the winding-holes preventing the insertion of the key until a cord is pulled or a trigger (or "bolt") moved aside, this simultaneously applying the spring-loading to keep the movement running. Hence the term "bolt-and-shutter maintaining-power" as applied to such fittings on early long-case clocks: and very occasionally the same device was applied to mantel clocks, although the short pendulums and verge escapement of these gave such rough-and-ready timekeeping that the unnecessary refinement of the bolt-and-shutter was merely the clockmaker boasting. Another device used to improve the quality of timekeeping was the second and a quarter pendulum. The standard one-second pendulum needs to be approximately thirty-nine inches long, and any minute adjustment for timekeeping can usually be made by screwing a wing-nut up or down on a screw-thread at the end of the pendulum rod, so making slight variation in the position of the brass-faced lead pendulum bob. If the pendulum could conveniently be lengthened then it would swing fewer times each minute and every hour, and if there is any error in length, as there is sure to be with the periodic changes of temperature, then it will not be magnified so much. A one-second pendulum swings the surprising number of 86,400 times every twenty-four hours, so the slightest error will be magnified that number of times. Somewhere about the year 1675, William Clement, one of the grand company of early makers and a contemporary of Robert Hooke and Isaac Newton, realised that a convenient portion of the hour for a clock movement would be a second and a quarter, instead of one second, and a pendulum to beat this time would need to be precisely 61·155 inches long—

a convenient length to accommodate in the conventional long-case trunk if the pendulum bob may swing close to the ground. Such a pendulum beats only forty-eight times a minute instead of sixty, so there is a considerable reduction in magnification of error.

But all such horological tricks were elementary. Errors of a second or more were not serious in a workaday world *sans* telephones, *sans* television, *sans* B.B.C. pips and the chimes of Big Ben. Most important makers sold their clocks together with a "dyall" (i.e. a sundial) to check the time, together with an equation table to show the relation between Sun time and Mean time. From this it is to be assumed that clocks were not often given sun-testing during the English winter, and the accuracy even from May to September was dependent on the vagaries of the English summer, with only a sundial as a corrective.

Errors of this magnitude were hopeless for astronomers, and when Charles II appointed Flamsteed Astronomer Royal, with a stipend of £100 a year, there were no clocks at Greenwich to make even elementary astronomical calculations reasonably accurate. Tompion built a set of clocks, one of which had a 13-foot pendulum (making a single beat in two seconds), and to reduce errors caused through winding, the movement was arranged to run for a year. After Flamsteed's death, and the consequent family squabbles about the clocks he had owned at Greenwich, they were taken by his widow and eventually sold. A few years ago a private collector discovered the "13-foot" clock in the vestry of a chapel near Greenwich. In some 250 years it had been taken out of its frame in the Greenwich Observatory Octagon room, fitted in a plain oak case, and of course converted to a one-second pendulum, though it still runs for a year. Mr. Courtenay Ilbert who now owns the clock does so with justifiable pride, as it is no doubt the original timepiece on which Greenwich Time was first recorded at Greenwich. Accurate identification is possible for, on account of the acrimonious disputes between the Royal Society and the Flamsteeds, the astronomer's name as well as that of Tompion are engraved on the dial, and the appearance of the dial tallies closely with the engraving of the Octagon Room from Flamsteed's own *Historia Coelestis*.

Wallace Nutting, the American writer on horology, points out that "It was natural that Britain, being an island, and therefore necessarily a maritime power, should devote more attention than other nations to chronometers. The reflex stimulus upon clockmaking in general is obvious." Much of course might be said with equal truth of Holland, and indeed Christiaan Huygens had proposed mounting a clock in gimbals: that other great envier of maritime greatness, Louis XIV, invited Huygens to Paris to demonstrate this new mechanism for finding longitude with precision. But the clock swung badly, and temperature changes at sea made the whole thing useless. Philip III of Spain had offered a large reward for a workable marine chronometer at the close of the sixteenth century, without avail, but

CHIMING MANTEL CLOCK WITH MOON-WORK
IN RED AND GOLD LACQUER CASE
Thomas Turner, *c.* 1760

By courtesy of the Trustees of the British Museum
ENGLISH WATCHES
Gold watch with outer case of carnelian. Made by Strigner for James II, *c.* 1687
(top and bottom left)
Enamelled and jewelled gold watch. David Bouquet, *fl.* 1628-65
(bottom centre)
Gold repeating watch in open-work case. Thomas Tompion and Edward Banger, 1701
(top and bottom right)

the promise of genius from English clockmakers induced the British Government in 1714 to offer the then very considerable sum of £10,000 for a method of ascertaining a craft's longitude at sea *to within one degree* on a voyage to the West Indies. The prize was to be increased to £20,000 if the clock gave longitude within thirty minutes, but such an accuracy was hardly considered possible (though now an everyday occurrence at sea and in the air), for thirty minutes of longitude correspond with two minutes of time—and it was never considered possible for a marine clock to err by less than two minutes after a six-weeks' journey to the Indies.

The prize was such an encouragement to British clockmakers that one, John Harrison, decided to give up his whole life to the task. He was a Yorkshire carpenter from Pontefract, and all his earliest clocks had wooden wheels. But on hearing of the £20,000 prize he came to London, at the age of thirty-five, bearing drawings of a timepiece which he felt would satisfy the Board of Longitude's requirements, and these drawings were eventually shown to George Graham. The advice Graham gave was probably encouraging. We have no written record. But Harrison went back to his job of making and repairing clocks, and spent the next seven years perfecting his marine chronometer. When he next came to London it was not only in search of the prize. He had determined to set up business with the London clockmakers, and took premises in Red Lion Square.

Halley the astronomer accompanied Harrison and George Graham on tests with the new "No. 1 Timekeeper" on a barge, and later the clock was used on a voyage across the Bay of Biscay to Lisbon. A navigational error of only five miles was shown on this occasion, a revolutionary degree of accuracy for those days thus having been achieved, and Harrison was awarded £500 as some encouragement for his work.

Britain's war with Spain prevented more tests being made for a considerable time, as it was feared Harrison's improved chronometer might be captured and duplicated by the enemy. There is a startling parallel here with the invention of the magnetron valve which produces very high-frequency pulses for radar, and also for electrical observatory timekeepers. Although the magnetron was urgently needed during the war, officials were fearful of using it lest the precious device were captured intact by the enemy; and as the magnetron is in a wall of steel it could not be detonated in an emergency. But Harrison's period of waiting was not one of idleness. In the waiting years he made improved versions of a marine chronometer now only five inches in diameter. By 1759, exactly thirty-one years after George Graham had seen the Yorkshireman's first drawings, the chronometer was ready for trials for the £20,000 prize. On the first voyage an error of only one and a half miles was achieved, such a startling degree of accuracy that the Board refused to pay out the award until further verification could be made. Three years of bickering ensued. The chronometer

HARRISON'S FOURTH MARINE CHRONOMETER, 1759
Winner of the Admiralty's £20,000 reward

was tried again, and then showed an error of less than one minute in five months' navigation on the high seas: and it is amusing now to record that the skipper of the *Deptford* used for these trials made an error in navigation which nearly ruined the whole test. After eighteen days at sea the skipper maintained his position as 13 degrees 50 minutes west of Portsmouth. The Harrison chronometers showed the position to be 15 degrees 19 minutes. If the chronometer were really so much in error it would be useless continuing the voyage, and the skipper was intent on putting back to port. Harrison's son, entrusted on this voyage with the precious timepiece, insisted that there was no error, so they sailed on and found Madeira next day as predicted by chronometer and calculation. That they did so, a news-letter of the times records, "was a matter of great relief to the ship's company, who were then in great scarcity of beer."

Quibbling between the Board, Harrison, the Astronomer Royal, and many officials, as well as rival clockmakers, was not at an end. £10,000 was paid in two instalments on account, but an appeal had to be made to George III for the final grant of £8,750, and Harrison never had the full benefit of the prize in his lifetime. Even after his death the wrangling went on, and his son and daughter even quarrelled about the inscription for his tombstone in Hampstead Church.

One of the quibblers was also a great clockmaker, Thomas Mudge. He was one of the first committee-men appointed to examine Harrison's chronometer in 1765. Mudge, a Graham apprentice, was son of a clergyman

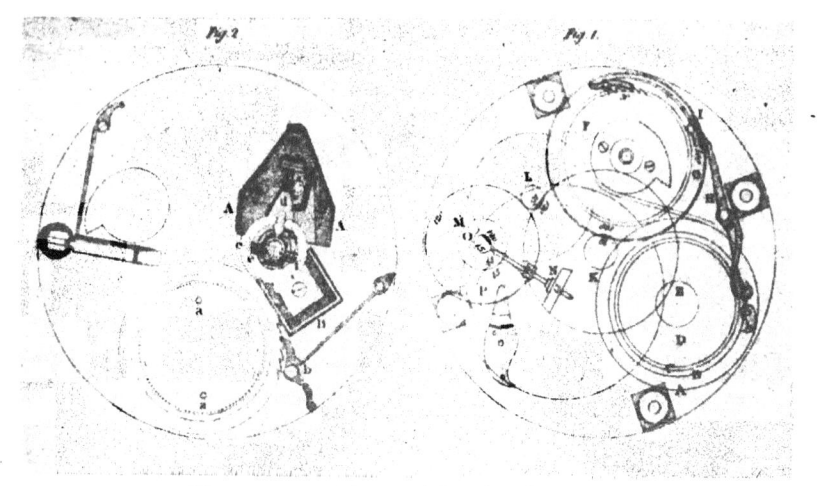

MOVEMENT OF THOMAS MUDGE'S TIMEKEEPER
Engraving from *A Description of the Timekeeper Invented by Mr. Thomas Mudge*, 1799

and schoolmaster in Exeter. After establishing a successful clock and watch business in London he set his heart on capturing the Longitude award. He did not, but he was paid some £3,000 for his trouble, and his marine chronometers were sent on voyages to Newfoundland under the care of Admiral Campbell. As in Harrison's case, the bickerings continued after the clockmaker's death. Mudge's son Thomas published in 1799 *A Description With Plates of The Timekeeper invented by Mr. Thomas Mudge*, with extracts of letters to the Astronomer Royal, Dr. Maskelyne, to the patron Count Bruhl, to Dutton (another famous clockmaker of Georgian times) and others in the controversy.

John Arnold and Thomas Earnshaw also determined to win part of the Longitude prize. Like Mudge, Arnold was a Westcountryman. So proud was he of his work that when asked to submit his "No. 1" chronometer for test he boasted to the Board: "I have made upwards of 900 chronometers, but never two alike so long as I can see room for any possible improvements. I have twenty No. 1 timepieces!" Like Mudge, again, he was eventually paid £3,000 for his discoveries, and on his second voyage in 1772 Captain Cook took Arnold's "No. 3" chronometer aboard the *Adventurer*. Thomas Earnshaw, a young watchmaker from Ashton-under-Lyne, at last in 1789 persuaded the Astronomer Royal to have one of the new chronometers tested. At the close of the eighteenth century Earnshaw was paid on encouraging £500, but he did not get the balance of £2,500 until 1803. The wrangling, again, continued, and *five years after* he had been given the balance, Earnshaw published an angry "Appeal to the Public" telling how he had been wronged!

Earnshaw taught some of his secrets of jewelling and precision work to William Frodsham, who though not the greatest of the pioneer chronometer craftsmen was probably the most prolific, and the firm of Frodsham's exists to-day, still setting a standard in craftsmanship. William Frodsham's first chronometer shop was in Red Lion Square, where he sold marine chronometers to the skippers of steamers plying from the Thames. The little shop was at its zenith in 1790, but between the years 1822 and 1835 the next generation of Frodshams was engaged in the pursuit of precision timekeeping of a far greater order than dreamed possible by the elder Frodsham or his contemporaries Earnshaw and Arnold. Greenwich tests in 1830 showed that one of the Frodsham chronometers gave an error of only 57/100ths of a second.

Twenty years later Edmund Denison Beckett, Q.C., whose profession was the law but whose hobby was horology, devised the gravity escapement for Big Ben's clock movement, and although this did not render the Graham dead-beat escapement obsolescent it did revolutionise turret-clock construction, and on becoming Baron Grimthorpe this amateur horologist carried on with his investigations into the free pendulum, the type of construction not liable to variation in timekeeping when the force of heavy winds, rain or snow is applied to the large hands of public clocks. Vulliamy, Dent and others were working along similar lines, but the next great step forward in British horology was made in 1895 when F. Hope-Jones made the first practical application of electricity to time-keeping. Fifty-five years previously the Scots inventor, Alexander Bain, had been granted a patent for an

VERGE WATCH MOVEMENTS
c. 1700
Mudge, Rogers and Weston

HARRISON'S FIRST MARINE TIMEKEEPER
Constructed 1729-1735

electric relay device to operate a number of dials from one master key-wound clock, and in 1843 a pendulum driven by an electro-magnet was described, and indeed his electric clock was just one of his notions developed in toying with the quest for perpetual motion. Electric power for his clock was obtained by Bain's sinking metal electrodes into moist earth underneath the clock, the potential difference being applied to the magnetic coil driving the pendulum.

Turret Clock Movement from St. Giles's Church, Cambridge
Originally designed for King's College, Cambridge, by William Clement, 1671

This device made no practical step forward in precision horology, but the invention of Hope-Jones's "Synchronome Remontoire," although primarily, like Bain's developed as a master-and-slave-dial system, did introduce a new principle of making alternate electric contact without checking pendulum motion. R. J. Rudd made the next step three years later when he developed the free pendulum getting its electro-magnetic impulse at zero position of swing, but his ideas were stillborn and there was a gap in this British development until the year 1921, when W. H. Shortt completed his experiments with the "hit-and-miss" synchroniser, and a test made at Edinburgh's Royal Observatory by Professor Sampson showed that the Shortt clock was superior to any other type of observatory clock then in use. Not only had a great step forward been made in the electrical drive and follow, but the whole pendulum mechanism was encased in a copper cylinder evacuated, so eliminating interference in the swing caused by stray air currents. The Shortt clock soon became the observatory standard, but in this chronicle of British timekeeping it is interesting to record that two of the greatest contributions have been made by amateurs—by Grimthorpe for the gravity 'scapement used in Big Ben and several other famous London public clocks, and now by Captain E. Craig who, working on the basic model of the Shortt clock, has devised what experts such as H. Alan Lloyd believe to be the only really free pendulum device in existence to-day.

In the Grimthorpe gravity 'scapement the early English clockmakers such as Clement, Harris, Tompion and Graham would have seen the fulfilment of their dreams—a high degree of accuracy attained by purely mechanical drive for a pendulum. They could never have contemplated the marvels of the Shortt and Craig electric clocks, with their errors of less than 0.002 seconds. Now even the twentieth-century workers on the electrically-driven pendulum observatory clocks are confounded by the onward surge of electric development. The clock craftsman of to-day is not an accurate cutter of clock wheels and pinions, but a handicraft man in the cutting of quartz-crystals, for now our latest clocks have no "works," no weights, no pendulum—and in some instances not even a dial but a cathode-ray tube screen as in a television or radar frame. They are driven by a quartz-crystal-controlled electric oscillator.

While the Royal Observatory still treasures its Shortt clocks (though regrettably having sold, a few years ago, its now priceless Arnold Nos. 1 and 2 Regulators, which had been made for £1,010 in 1774 and are now historic), transit time to-day is checked not by pendulums but by high-frequency electric oscillations. The whole mechanism is an application of electronics to horology, and is akin to the oscillating-crystal drive used to keep B.B.C. broadcasting stations rigidly to their allotted wavelengths, and to the radar mechanism used to time world-record flights of jet-propelled aircraft. It is a fascinating new chapter, and a great credit to British inventors, notably those at the National Physical Laboratory, and the

Royal Aircraft Establishment at Farnborough. But it is, so the old craftsmen would feel, not clockmaking. It may be electronics, and the triumph of brain over craftsmanship. The world has rushed ahead too far from the day when, as Aristophanes told us, man measured the hour by the number of times his shadow was greater than the length of his own feet. For 350 years until the Victorian era of mass-production, we made fine clocks. Now, in our observatory devices which tell time to within one-thousandth of a second, we make good electronics. But that's another story.

JOHN HILDERSON'S SIGNATURE

SHORT BIBLIOGRAPHY

Observations on the History and Practice of the Art of Watchmaking (*Archaeologia*, vol. xxxiii, 1849), by Octavius Morgan.—*Curiosities of Clocks and Watches*, 1866, by Edward J. Wood.—*A Handbook and Directory of Old Scottish Clockmakers from 1540 to 1850* A.D., 1904, by John Smith.—*English Domestic Clocks*, 1913, by Herbert Cescinsky and Malcolm R. Webster. Routledge.—*Chats on Old Clocks and Watches*, 1917, by Arthur Hayden. Fisher Unwin.—*The Marine Chronometer*, 1923, by Rupert T. Gould.—*Some Clocks and Jacks, with Notes on the History of Horology* (*Archaeologia*, vol. lxxvii, 1928, by R. P. Howgrave-Graham.—*Watches: their History, Decoration and Mechanism*, 1929, by G. H. Baillie. Methuen.—*Old English Clocks and Watches and their Makers*, 6th ed., 1933, by F. J. Britten. Spon.—*The Old English Master Clockmakers and their Clocks*, 1938, by Herbert Cescinsky. Routledge.—*The Evolution of the Long-case Clock* and other articles in *The Antique Collector* (from 1940 onwards), by Percy Dawson